Native Americans

Iroquois Indians

Caryn Yacowitz

Heinemann Library
Chicago, Illinois

© 2003 Heinemann Library
a division of Reed Elsevier Inc.
Chicago, Illinois

Customer Service 888-454-2279

Visit our website at www.heinemannlibrary.com

Photo research by Alan Gottlieb.
Printed and bound in the United States by Lake Book Manufacturing, Inc.

07 06 05
10 9 8 7 6 5 4 3 2

Library of Congress Cataloging-in-Publication Data
Yacowitz, Caryn.
  Iroquois Indians / Caryn Yacowitz.
    v. cm. -- (Native Americans)
Includes bibliographical references and index.
Contents: Forests and lakes -- The beginnings of the Iroquois -- People of the longhouse -- Iroquois villages -- Farming, hunting, and fishing -- Wampum -- Buckskin clothing -- Families and clans -- Religion, medicine, and spirits -- An Iroquois creation story -- Iroquois games -- Early settlers -- The land is taken -- The Iroquois today.
  ISBN 1-40340-303-1 (lib. bdg.) -- ISBN 1-40340-510-7 (pbk.)
  1. Iroquois Indians--Juvenile literature. [1. Iroquois Indians. 2. Indians of North America.] I. Title. II. Native Americans (Heinemann Library (Firm))
  E99.I7 Y23 2002
  974.004'9755--dc21
                        2002006323

Acknowledgments
The author and publisher are grateful to the following for permission to reproduce copyright material: pp. 4, 5 James Randklev/The Image Bank/Getty Images; pp. 6, 15, 30T Iroquois Indian Museum, Howes Cave, NY; p. 7 Rochester Museum and Science Center, Neg.#MR616; pp. 8, 20 Astor, Lenox and Tilden Foundations, General Research Division, New York Public Library; pp. 10, 14 Marilyn "Angel" Wynn/Nativestock; p. 11 The Granger Collection; pp. 12, 21 John Kahionhes Fadden; p. 13 Rochester Museum and Science Center, Neg.#MR1061; p. 16 John Bigelow Taylor/Art Resource; p. 17 Canadian Museum of Civilization; p. 18 Heinemann Library; p. 19 National Museum of the American Indian, Smithsonian Institution; p. 22 Rochester Museum and Science Center, Neg.#MR545; p. 23 Kennan Ward/Corbis; p. 24 Notman Photographic Archives, McCord Museum of Canadian History, Montreal; p. 25 National Museum of the American Indian, Smithsonian Institution, Neg.#N15337; p. 26 National Archives of Canada; p. 27 John Carter Brown Library, Brown University; p. 28 Library of Congress; p. 29 Department of Library Services, American Museum of Natural History, Neg#273540; p. 30B Catherine Leroy/Sipa Press.

Cover photograph by Nathan Benn/Corbis.

 Special thanks to Rita Chrisjohn Benson for her help in the preparation of this book.

Some words are shown in bold, **like this.** You can find out what they mean by looking in the glossary.

Contents

Forests and Lakes

Long ago, thick forests covered parts of present-day New York, Pennsylvania, Ohio, and southeast Canada. The forests had elm, maple, **birch,** cedar, and other trees. The many clear lakes and rivers were filled with fish. Deer, **elk,** bears, beavers, and wild turkeys lived here.

Most of the trees lost their leaves each fall. Winters were cold and snowy. Summers were hot and humid. Wild berries, fruits, and herbs grew in meadows and along streams. The soil in this area was very **fertile**.

PACIFIC
OCEAN

NORTH
AMERICA

ATLANTIC
OCEAN

N
W E
S

0   450 mi
0   725 km

GULF OF
MEXICO

Iroquois
League territory

The Beginnings of the Iroquois

Many years ago, the **tribes** living in this area were at war with one another. Then, a **holy** man came from the north. The Indians called this man Peacemaker. He told the tribes that if they stopped fighting and joined together, they could have peace. Peacemaker and a man named Hiawatha spread the news about peace.

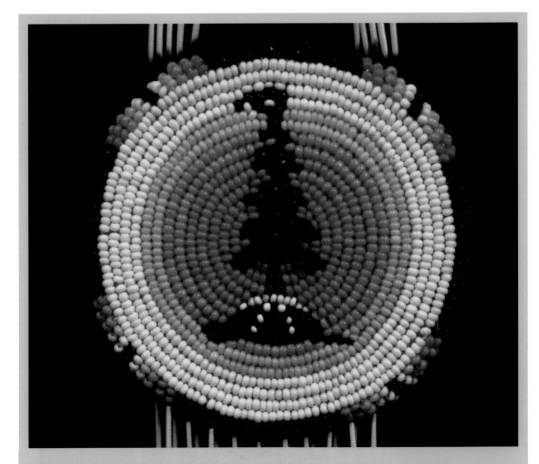

*This **medallion** shows the Great Tree of Peace where the tribes buried their weapons.*

Five tribes joined together. They formed a government called the Iroquois **League.** They were the Seneca, Cayuga, Onondaga, Oneida, and Mohawk tribes. To show they wanted peace, they took a tall white pine tree out of the ground. They tossed their **weapons** into the hole where the tree had been and planted the tree again. They called it the Great Tree of Peace. The tree was a **symbol** of **union** for the tribes.

This painting shows Peacemaker and Hiawatha talking to a leader named Thadodado. When they started talking, Thadodado did not want peace. Later, he agreed to be part of the Iroquois League.

The Great Tree of Peace

The roots of the Great Tree of Peace spread in four directions. This showed that peace and law were offered to other people. The Iroquois say that an eagle sat on top of the tree. With its sharp eyes, the eagle watched in all directions. It screamed if peace was in danger. Fifty tribal leaders sat under the Great Tree of Peace. There they made the Great Law for the Iroquois League.

People of the Longhouse

The five **tribes** called themselves the Haudenosaunee (pronounced "Ho-den-O-show-nee"). The name means "people of the longhouse." They used this name for two reasons. They lived in houses that were very long. The tribes also thought of themselves as spread out over the land, like a long house of people.

This drawing shows a group of Iroquois leaders talking about the Great Law.

French **explorers** called the Haudenosaunee the *Iroquois*. Today, both names are used. In the 1720s, the Tuscarora tribe joined the Iroquois **League**. The Tuscaroras came from the area of present-day North and South Carolina. They had been forced off their land by white **settlers**. That made six nations in the Iroquois League.

Tribal Names

The Senecas were called "Keepers of the Western Door" of the longhouse. The Mohawks were "Keepers of the Eastern Door." The Onondagas were "Keepers of the Fire" because they lived in the center of the house, where the fire burns. This was also where the central government of the Iroquois League met.

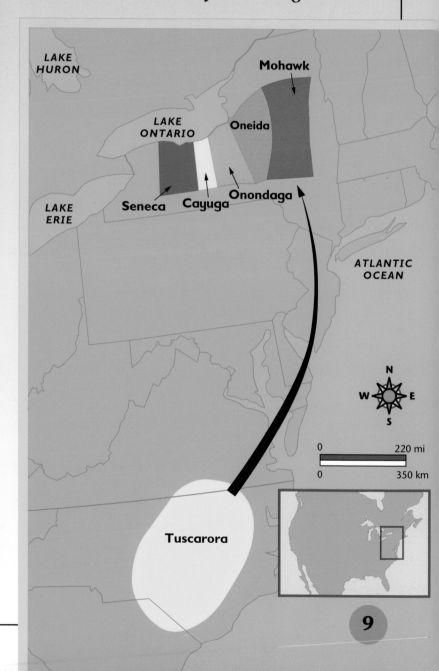

Iroquois Villages

The Iroquois people cut clearings in the forest for their villages. For **protection,** they built high fences. Longhouses were built inside the fences. Most longhouses were between 60 and 150 feet (18 to 46 meters) long. One very old longhouse was more than 400 feet (122 meters) long. Longhouses were made from a frame of **sapling** poles covered with elm bark. A door was at each end. There were no windows, but there were fire holes in the roof so smoke could escape from the cooking fires.

Iroquois longhouses look like this on the inside.

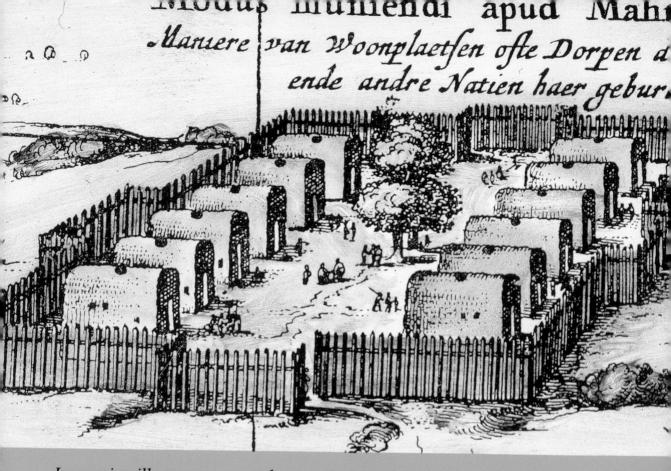

Iroquois villages were made up of many longhouses grouped together. The high fences protected the village.

Many families lived in each longhouse. The families were all members of the same **clan.** The clan animal was often drawn over the doors. This was like a welcome sign for visitors from other villages who were from the same clan. Long, braided **husks** of corn hung from the **rafters.** Dried beans, clothing, tools, toys, and **weapons** were stored on shelves along the walls. There were also shelves for sleeping. People slept on corn husk mats.

Farming, Hunting, and Fishing

The Iroquois people were farmers. Women did most of the farming. Fields of corn, beans, and squash surrounded Iroquois villages. These crops were called the Three Sisters. The Iroquois grew many different kinds of corn. Corn soup was an important food. Corn was used in Iroquois **ceremonies.** Different parts of the corn plant were used to make medicine, dolls, baskets, pipes, and sleeping mats.

This painting by Iroquois artist John Fadden shows the Three Sisters: corn, beans, and squash.

This painting, "The Bowmaker," is by Iroquois artist Ernest Smith. He painted in the 1930s, but he wanted to show the way that bows may have been made by Iroquois in the past.

The Iroquois used bow and arrows and, later, guns to hunt. They hunted deer, **elk,** rabbits, bears, and other animals. The Iroquois did not have horses. They hunted on foot. They caught wild turkeys, geese, and pigeons in traps. They used elm bark **canoes** to fish in the rivers and lakes. The Iroquois collected maple syrup and gathered wild berries, nuts, and fruits.

Strawberry Medicine

The Iroquois called strawberries a food of the **spirit** because they are heart-shaped. The leaves were used to cure pains. Today, strawberries are still celebrated with a special **ceremony**.

13

Wampum

Wampum is the name of white and purple beads made by the Iroquois. **Whelk** shells and **quahog** shells were cut and drilled to make *wampum* beads. The beads were then sewn into special *wampum* belts. The belts recorded agreements between the **tribes.** They also recorded **treaties** between the tribes and **settlers.** The *wampum* belts had **woven symbols** or pictures. Special people in the tribe knew how to read the symbols.

This quahog shell has wampum beads inside it. Wampum was made from quahog and whelk shells.

This is a copy of the Hiawatha Wampum. *The real belt is* **sacred** *to the Iroquois people.*

The Hiawatha *Wampum,* also called The Five Nation *Wampum* Belt, is one of the most important *wampum* belts. It shows the five tribes of the first Iroquois **League.** The four rectangles are symbols of four tribes. The symbol in the middle is the Onondaga tribe. It is shown as the Great Tree of Peace, where the most important government was located. The five tribes are connected by a line of white beads to show their **union.** The line going out on each side shows that more tribes can join the Iroquois League.

Buckskin Clothing

The Iroquois wore clothing made of tanned deerskin called buckskin. Women and girls wore long skirts or dresses and blouses. Sometimes they wore **leggings.** Men and boys wore a kind of short skirt and leggings. Everyone wore moccasins. The Iroquois decorated clothing and shoes with beads and dyed porcupine **quills.** They also dyed moose hair blue, red, or yellow and used it to decorate clothing. Both men and women wore their hair in braids. Some men removed all their hair except for a strip down the middle of their heads. Today, this hairstyle is called a mohawk.

This beaded bag was made in the 1830s. It is now on display at the Fenimore Art Museum in Cooperstown, New York.

All Iroquois people wore moccasins. Someone worked very hard to sew the beaded designs on this pair.

In the winter, the Iroquois people wore snowshoes. Snowshoes helped them travel quickly, even in deep snow. When the Iroquois started to meet white **settlers,** they traded animal skins for cloth, glass beads, and silver. The Iroquois soon began to use glass beads and silver for decoration.

Families and Clans

Every Iroquois is a member of a **clan.** Clans are like big families who are all related to the same woman **ancestor.** Children are the same clan as their mother. In each village, the oldest women of each clan were the clan mothers. The clan mothers chose the **tribal** leaders, who were called *sachems.* The clans are named for animals. There are Turtle, Bear, Wolf, Hawk, Deer, and Beaver clans, as well as many others.

These are **symbols** for some of the Iroquois clans.

*This is a photograph of an Iroquois family in the early 1900s. At that time, many Iroquois did not wear **traditional** clothing.*

Boys learned to hunt and fish from their fathers. Mothers taught girls how to prepare animal skins, farm, cook, and take care of the younger children. The Iroquois treated their children well. They never spanked children. When a child was very bad, an adult threw water in the child's face.

Religion, Medicine, and Spirits

The Iroquois believe in the Great **Spirit,** who created the world. They also believe in good spirits and evil spirits. A group of people called the False Face Society helps heal sickness. They cut wooden masks from living trees. These are called False Face Masks. They are worn to scare away evil spirits. Because the masks are **sacred,** the Iroquois believe they should be seen only by other Iroquois. Other masks are made from corn **husks.** These are called Husk Face Masks.

These are Husk Face dancers. They are dancing in the Midwinter Festival.

20

Iroquois artist John Fadden painted this picture of an eagle dancer. The eagle dance is an important Iroquois ceremony.

The Iroquois hold **festivals** to celebrate crops, seasons, and events. The Strawberry **Ceremony** and the Midwinter Festival are held every year. During the Midwinter Festival, the Iroquois play games and give the Thanksgiving Address. This speech asks people to respect the earth and live in peace with all creatures.

The Iroquois Creation Story

The Iroquois people tell a story about the beginning of the world. Long ago, there was only water, with the Sky World above it. A great *sachem* in the Sky World took a tree out of the ground. His wife, Sky Woman, fell through the hole. As Sky Woman fell, swans flew under her. They held her on their wings. The animals in the water watched Sky Woman fall. They knew she could not swim. They decided to create land for her.

In this painting, the Iroquois artist Ernest Smith presents an Iroquois belief about how life was created.

In the Iroquois creation story, North America rests on the back of a turtle.

Muskrat brought mud up from the bottom of the sea. He put the mud on Turtle's back to create land. The land became North America. The animals called it Turtle Island. The birds put Sky Woman on Turtle Island. There, she walked in a circle, dropping the seeds she had brought with her from the Sky World. The seeds grew into the Three Sisters, wild strawberries, and all the other plants. The story of Sky Woman's fall is remembered today in the Iroquois Women's Dance.

Iroquois Games

The game of stickball was created by Indians. Long ago, the Iroquois played stickball dring **religious ceremonies.** Hundreds of people played the game. One game could cover an area 20 miles (32 kilometers) long. The games lasted many days. Only men played this rough game. Two teams played. They used wooden rackets and a ball made from deerskin or wood. The Iroquois liked to bet on which team would win.

*This photograph of an Iroquois **lacrosse** team was taken in Canada in 1867. Modern lacrosse comes from Indian stickball.*

These Iroquois people are playing a game of peach pit.

"Snow snake" is another Iroquois game. First, a log is dragged through the snow to make a path. The "snakes" are long, straight sticks from a **hickory** tree. The winner is the team that throws its sticks the farthest along the icy path. Men and women played other games such as the peach pit game. This is a game of chance. It is played as part of the Midwinter **Festival.**

Early Settlers

In the 1600s, white **settlers** and **explorers** came to the area of the Iroquois **League**. The Iroquois traded with the settlers. In the 1700s, Benjamin Franklin and Thomas Jefferson were leaders in the American **colonies**. They respected the Iroquois government. In 1754, Franklin invited Iroquois *sachems* to a meeting called the Albany Plan of **Union**. The *sachems* taught colonial leaders about the Great Law. Franklin and Jefferson thought the colonies should have a law like the Great Law.

This Mohawk sachem explained the Great Law to the colonists. His name was Tee Yee Neen Ho Ga Row.

The English gave a medal to the Iroquois who fought on their side during the Revolutionary War.

Franklin and Jefferson also wanted the colonies to be free from England. The colonies fought the Revolutionary War to be free from England. The Iroquois had to decide whether to fight for England or for the colonies. The Iroquois League decided each **tribe** should choose for itself. The Oneida and Tuscarora tribes fought for the colonies. The other tribes fought for England.

The Land Is Taken

After the Revolutionary War, the United States government took much of the land from the Iroquois people. In 1784, the **Treaty** of Fort Stanwick made the Iroquois give up thousands of acres of land. Many Iroquois people were starving. An Iroquois leader named Joseph Brandt helped many Iroquois people **settle** in Canada. A law passed in 1835 forced other Iroquois to leave their homeland and live in present-day Oklahoma. Iroquois children were taken from their families and put into Indian schools. There, they were punished if they spoke the Iroquois language.

The Mohawk leader Thayendanegea was also known by the name Joseph Brandt.

*It is said that the **Spirit** of the Corn told Handsome Lake how the Iroquois people should live.*

Handsome Lake was an Iroquois leader who gave his people hope at this sad time. He said Iroquois dances, **ceremonies,** stories, and crafts would make the people strong again. He warned them not to drink alcohol or follow other bad habits of the settlers. His **religion** is called the Handsome Lake Religion, or the Longhouse Religion. Many Iroquois people practice the Longhouse Religion today.

Iroquois Today

Today there are about 80,000 Iroquois living in the United States and Canada. They live in nineteen different communities, mostly in the northeastern United States. The Iroquois people follow their **traditions.** They work as teachers, lawyers, nurses, doctors, and artists. Some men of the Mohawk **tribe** have worked building skyscrapers all over the United States. Mohawk ironworkers helped build the World Trade Center. They also helped with rescue efforts at the World Trade Center after the terrorist attacks on September 11, 2001.

Glossary

ancestor relative who lived long before someone's parents and grandparents

birch tree with thin, smooth bark

canoe narrow boat pushed along with paddles

ceremony event that celebrates a special occasion

clan group of families that are related

colony land that is ruled by a distant country

elk large animal that looks like a deer but is much bigger

explorer person who travels to find out more about a place or region

fertile good for growing crops

festival day or time of celebration

hickory tall tree with strong, hard wood

holy very religious

husk dry covering of a cob of corn

lacrosse ball game played today with long-handled wooden rackets

league groups joined together to help one another

legging covering for the leg

medallion round decoration that looks like a medal

protect keep from harm or danger

quahog (you say "CO-hog") kind of clam with a white and purple shell

quill long, stiff spine that sticks out on the body of a porcupine

rafter large, sloping piece of wood that holds up a roof

religion system of spiritual beliefs and practices

sacred holy; something that has special meaning for a community or tribe

sapling young, thin tree

settle make a home in a new place. A person who does this is a settler.

spirit invisible force or being with special power

symbol something that stands for something else

tradition custom or story that has been passed from older people to younger people for a long time

treaty agreement between governments or groups of people

tribe group of people who share language, customs, beliefs, and often government

union number of nations or groups of people joined together

weapon thing used for fighting, such as a sword or gun

weave lace together threads or other material

whelk large sea snail

More Books to Read

Englar, Mary. *The Iroquois: The Six Nation Confederacy*. Minnetonka, Minn.: Capstone Press, Incorporated, 2002.

Kalman, Bobbie. *Life in a Longhouse Village*. New York: Crabtree Publishing Company, 2001.

Levine, Ellen. *If You Lived with the Iroquois*. New York: Scholastic, Incorporated, 1999.

Ryan, Marla (Ed.). *Tribes of Native America: Iroquois and Mohawk*. Farmington, Mich.: Gale Group, 2002.

Index